The Dedalus Press

Travels With Gandolpho

Eva Bourke

TRAVELS WITH GANDOLPHO

EVA BOURKE

The Dedalus Press
24 The Heath ~ Cypress Downs ~ Dublin 6W
Ireland

© Eva Bourke and The Dedalus Press, 2000

Cover Design by Miriam de Búrca

ISBN 1 901233 60 X (paper)
ISBN 1 901233 61 8 (bound)

Acknowledgements:
Poetry Ireland Review; Chapman; ROPES; Thee Shop; The Stinging Fly; Éigse na gCúige; Poetry Now 2000 Anthology; NUIG Women's Studies Review — where some of these poems were published.

Dedalus Press books are represented and distributed in the U.S.A. and Canada by **Dufour Editions Ltd.**, P.O. Box 7, Chester Springs, Pennsylvania 19425
in the UK by **Central Books**, 99 Wallis Road, London E9 5LN

The Dedalus Press receives financial assistance from
An Chomhairle Ealaíon, The Arts Council, Ireland.
Printed in Dublin by Colour Books Ltd

*... at night we dance in front of the statue of beasts
dressed in scales, feathers, carapace and skin
the litany of our misdeeds is endless
kindly spirits don't reject us
we have strayed among oceans and stars too long
receive us who are tired beyond measure
into your herd*
— Zbigniew Herbert

*Miracle — just look around:
the world ever-present.*

*An extra miracle, just as everything is extra:
what is unthinkable
is thinkable.*
— Wislawa Szymborska

for Eoin

Contents

Bulletin	9
Cutting Hair	10
In Memory of J.M.	12
Letter from the Danube	14
Rhinoceros	17
Dinner with Gandolpho	25
Isodorus	26
Ménage	29
In the Little Building	31
Letter to Sujata	34
Oedipus and the Sphinx	38
On Forgetting	40
Some Days	48
The Art Judges	50
Angels and Devils	52
The Spider	55
The Unicorn	57
June 18, 1998	60
Valse Triste	64
Ballade	66
Travels with Gandolpho	69
Gandolpho's Moods	71
Circus	72
In Duiche Iar	77
Berlin Notebook	80
Notes	92

BULLETIN

The master of trance is coming to town:
I throw in my lot with the crows
in their dizzy lofts.

Where green dust covers the tree tops
feathers drip now and then
from crowded gallery seats.

There's freedom in falling: feathers,
eggshells, ourselves,
let fall by God-knows whose hand.

Out of dark houses we've come
blinded into a wing span of light,
the new grass provides easy seats.

All halls are fully booked
for the dazzling master's premiere.
We use our lives daily like pencils

that grow shorter and blunter
for this one brief untitled
mortal sketch

which we fold over and over,
let it take wing,
let it fall wherever it will.

Cutting Hair

Having done this so often, I could do it blind-
folded, by touch only. My fingertips
have a memory of their own, they'd find
the temporal bone, following its dip
from buckled ridge to ear, which as
I'd know well, even though I wouldn't see,
would be damp and flushed after your bath
and running into a transparent ivory

just below where the outer rim curves like a flat-
tened shell around the inner rim,
the fleshy lobe as soft as fleece or velvet.
That's where I'd begin: this is the spot
where utmost concentration is required, not
one nick of the epidermis, no drawing blood
with the sharp points of the instrument's allowed
as I'd pick up wet curls one by one, wondering

if your hair's gone a little greyer again
and if the fine frizz on your neck
which I'd clip back closer to the skin
just above the cerebral vertebrae
is taking on the sheen of glacial firn
or new frost on a winter tree.
Slowly I would run my fingers up
and over the back and sides of your head

letting them spell out the lines
and marks like braille, telling signs
of a life lived fifty years and more:
those creases, that mole, this boyhood scar,
all intimately known, familiar
tokens of experience, tolerance and wit,
and lifting each strand between
the thumb and index finger of my right

I'd gauge them at roughly four inches length
before I'd let the scissors do their job
of taking years off you, and cuttings drop.
You've given yourself into my hands
the warm skull beneath your still
plentiful hair, heavy and fragile,
the sutures' crazy zigzag lines
knitting together the cranial bones

that contain so much of you, my love
that's indispensable and precious to us both,
all rendered with entire trust and calm
to me and the work in hand. For a time
I hold the scales that tip to pleasure or to pain
before we go out in the January rain
leaving behind us little piles of hair
as gleaming offerings on the bathroom floor.

IN MEMORY OF J.M. (1932 - 1997)

> *Wir haben keinen Grund.*
> *Bewunderung und Liebe oder Haß*
> *dem Tod zu zeigen, den ein Maskenmund*
> *tragischer Klage wunderlich entstellt.*
> *Noch ist die Welt voll Rollen, die wir spielen.*
> R.M. Rilke

Thinking about Jack, I remember he wrote
that sometimes when he left the pub and walked out
into Dominick Street, stopping for a while
below the rain-glazed lamps,
letting the cars float past
in the unbreathable November air
that made him feel he was inside a fish tank
with fingerprint-smudged walls,

or on late summer evenings when the sun
flood-lit the canals and enlisted
every window, every bit of metal and glass
in its heliography, that he thought he had chanced
into the middle of a play, negotiating his entrance
through the wings onto a bright stage
where props lay piled up in the corners,
where extras were numerous and the scenes changed fast

and suddenly he felt the spotlights were on him
as he sauntered from one side of the street
to the other, a small lively figure, anorak-clad
with a shoulder bag of seditious poems and songs,

cap askew, hands deep in his pockets,
he came under the scrutiny of an almighty director
calling from somewhere: Hey you, you there in the green parka,
go back and do that walk across the stage again!

I see him standing, musing, mischievous, a little
contrary, prickly like his country's emblem,
not given to obeying just any direction; he hums a tune
or thinks up a cutting-edge line, preferably in the face
of the powerful, and I, too, want to call: Hey Jack,
come back and walk across the street again!
He jaunties up his cap as he would when a joke, a song
or a poem pleased him and sets off on his way.

But when he left for good through a gap in the backdrop
while we were busy playing our parts,
playing them haphazardly, greedy for applause,
careless of death's distorted clownish face,
the light that fell in through that gap
changed suddenly into real light,
the air we breathed turned into real air,
trees into real trees, rustling with leaves.

We do our routines, speak our lines deadpan
or ham up our acts performing to the galleries,
but his having wandered off the stage
leaving the crew of us players on our own
stops us in our tracks and brings us face to face
with the bare mise en scène of its truth
that for a moment we forget praise and curtain call
and plunge into acting out our lives wholly, body and soul.

Letter From The Danube

This year the swallows didn't arrive.
Who knows what might be the cause of that?

Always perfectly timed
when the sun strikes up its fanfare
and the river flows broad and calm
between green banks,

when orchards stand sunstruck for days
in a slow white hum
and vineyards and cornfields
wait for a breeze to stir their music,

that's when the swallows return.
Out of the blue first one
then a second envoy materialises
on poles or wires to scout the familiar haunts,

then the rank and file close behind them
pour from a gap in the sky,
down and down to fan out over the field,
travel-worn, brisk and full of chat as you too would be,

safe and at rest at last after a journey
across salt deserts, man-made traps
and the night of flaming oil fields,
with no other guide

but your small tough heart
and a memory
fixed bright as a star chart
in your mind.

The swallows are back. Each spring
I welcome them from the bridge,
reassured, even relieved.
But this year

the airstrips and stop-overs
between stable and hay barns are empty.
Little adobe nests stuck into ceiling nooks
like crumbling stucco — empty.

Pub hallways where swallows
swung in and out to feed their young,
Aztec house clusters mortared with swallow spit
and glued to rafters of grain lofts — all are silent.

On flyways above alders and pines — nothing.
Kite-winds lift off empty-handed.
No one scales the steep June sky.
Where are the swallows,

frock-coated mobsters,
debonair in shirtfront and cap
as they scissor through midge-webs
above the bean rows,

or cut across the river in the nick of a storm?
Which freak current
carried them off course?
What toxins blew their way?

Did they drop — little ones first —
like cinders into the furnace of a desert?
Are they still lost drifting in icy spaces
looking for somewhere to rest?

This is a bad year — put on hold
until the swallows arrive looping and sliding
together on their breezy slide
to their nests and rich mid-air pickings.

Until the swallows arrive
the heart of the summer stops beating,
the river stands still
beneath a plague of flies that waft and breed

a dark spreading cloud
while in the unlit depths newt and slug fatten.

Rhinoceros

I

(From an Alexandrian manuscript)

I am Alia, the cook, the only survivor —

From the camel drivers
who hung around our vestibule
smoked water pipes and discussed sightings
of two-headed serpents, winged lions,
I first heard of a powerful beast with one single horn.
I know now these events were omens
of the war in the North,
the fever epidemic and the many dead.
If I'd paid more attention I would have seen
fingernails turning blue
or skin pulling off legs, like stockings,
birds that fell from the sky.

Nearby signposts were back to front,
we knew neither time nor day
nor where in hell we could go.

One night I put on my silk yashmak
crossed the courtyard's cool tiles
lay down under the tamarisk behind the house
pressed my ear to the ground and waited
for the touch of black pinions, of bird claws,

for the thunder of the monoceros approaching
through night thickets.

II

The rhino is in the infirmary.
The Pierrot
and several masked figures
are attending to it.
Apologies to Dürer
for missing the appointment again.

III

In the year 1513
the mighty king Emmanuel
displayed such an animal
to the gentlemen and ladies of his court.
It so terrified many
they fainted and had to be carried out into the air.
Its name is Rhinoceros.

IV

It is a tiny creature
because of the lowliness
of its incarnation.

Learn from it
for it is mild
and its heart is humble.

V

There's nothing more pitiful
than a sick rhinoceros
in a circus:
bulk without energy
in a curved non-Euclidean space.

VI

Dürer is tired of Holy Families,
the Holy Family with the Cricket,
the Holy Family with the Hare,
the Holy Family resting with the Blackbird,
of all the Marys in amalfi-blue cloaks
swaddling the Divine Infant,
not to speak of the passions,
martyrs and apocalypses,
seven-headed dragons, horned lambs,
Babylonian whores,
and the foursomes, the Riders,
Wind Angels, Bugle Angels,
the endless sieges and battles scenes.

But today he is filled with new spirit
having just heard about the rhinoceros.
A Dutch sailor who is lodging at the Golden Unicorn
gave an accurate description.
Dürer questions him for two hours
notes down all the details and begins
a preliminary sketch.
The house is quiet,
everyone's gone to a hamlet near Nuremberg
for the wedding of the cook's daughter.
He contemplates the paraphernalia
in his printing studio,
the presses, needles, knives, copperplates,
acid bottles, gums and inks,
uncertain which technique he should use —
etching, drypoint, engraving —
then decides on a woodcut
for something so imaginary and palpable.
This is how we've come to know it:
The colour of a speckled tortoise,
a body encased in thick shells
and of equal height as the elephant,
four squat chain-mail legs
that stand their ground
but can move rapidly, too,
a thick pelt infested with parasites,
a dewlapped chin full of bristles,
a single horn which is constantly sharpened on rocks,
and a crafty upward look from one small eye.

Dürer works in the Italianate blue of twilight.
A cricket behind the wall panels
turns its grinder,
outside a blackbird's sweet cantabile
calls in the night.
Suddenly above the smell of ink
and wood shavings in the studio
there's the stink of rhinoceros.

VII

If the earth were
the centre of the universe,
its own centre and navel
would be the stone rhinoceros
beside the Natural History Museum in Boston.

VIII

An ointment of unicorn's liver
mixed with egg yolks cures leprosy.

A belt made from unicorn skin
prevents fever and the plague.

Shoes of unicorn hide
ensure healthy feet.

The King of the Grail, Amfortas, suffered a wound
that could only be cured
with the help of a unicorn's heart
and the carbuncle which grows beneath its horn.

No animal will drink from a pool
before a unicorn has dipped
its horn into the water to test its purity.

Never eat at a banquet
unless you have a fragment of unicorn's horn
as a poison detector with you.

Alternatively you can put a unicorn's hoof
under your plate.

If it begins to heat up and smoke
don't touch a morsel of your food.

Wine tastes sweetest
from a golden unicorn cup
set with diamonds and pearls,

and if you want your medicines to work
you must buy them in pharmacies
with the sign of the unicorn.

IX

If you ever make the holy trek
through the desert to Mecca,
don't mind the sacred stone
or other manifestations of the prophet,
all that can come later;
head straight through the archway
behind the mosque.
In a walled-in orange grove
you will find two young unicorns
with curly manes and black horns.

X

The unicorn is more warm than cold.
Its staple foods are only the purest herbs.
It is notoriously shy of people,
especially of men.
Once a philosopher and a zoologist
pursued a unicorn
which leapt away from them in great leaps.
It came across a group of young girls
making daisy chains,
stopped, sat on its hindlegs
and stared in great wonder
at these beardless creatures
who seemed to be human all the same.
The philosopher and the zoologist
seized their chance and captured it.

Therefore if you want to catch unicorns
don't forget to bring a young girl with you.
It's of even greater advantage
to keep several in reserve.

XI

It lives on Prospero's island
in the cedar woods beside a lake
often stands on the banks
when the moon is out
and gazes at its own milk white reflection
its mild head with the startling horn
in the water's black mirror.

Dinner With Gandolpho

Paprika, a red rag
to any bull in a kitchen,
reminds me how you used to fly into rages
and of our hot German winter soups.

If the world were made of cinammon,
we'd see it as a light brown muffled fog.
All that sweetness would probably kill us.

Curry, immersed in post-colonial studies,
will have nothing to do with your snobbery
and middle-class pretensions,
as anyone from round here will tell you.

Pepper has an entirely ironic flavour.
We avoid it like the plague,
knowing what mayhem it can cause.

Saying that vanilla is a young girl in a miniskirt,
proves you're as drunk as a judge.
Just remember, we stole both Americas
for a whiff of that aroma.

Say what you like:
the world is concentrated in a taste bud,
not going at breakneck speed
over the four edges of the cosmos.

Isidorus

Isidorus — skinny, beard like a cloud —
takes us out to pasture.
We graze the rocky terrain, the deserts,
our hungry shadows move along cliff tops.

Isidorus drives us across motorways,
from the rivers of Babylon
to the roof-gardens
of Chicago, Hong Kong.

On flushed glass pinnacles we stand,
gaze at the plains' airstrips or out to sea,
to atolls that emerge from smog,
volcanic islands fizzing over with becquerels.

We rest our scale-covered bodies on concrete.
In the manner of high-minded ideas
that have become unmanageable
we've grown too many teeth and claws.

We are encumbered with weapons,
ranged-out tanks in an arms dump,
our use went in the crossfire
of a thousand screens.

We almost forgot there were miracles:
Long ago the wind played music in trees,
when the phoenix collected herbs — verbena,
love-in-a-mist, myrrh, bergamot, lavender —

for their sweet flames, then rose
singing with the sun,
pinions redder than gold.
It was a daily occurrence.

Flocks of winged horses
were more commonplace than starlings,
the great snake devoured itself regularly
like the cosmos,

unicorns stepped from the birch woods
at the beck and call of young girls,
sphinx and griffin served
as caretakers in the cities of the dead.

Envoys of many gods first,
then of one,
omens, threats, disasters,
those were our briefs.

We walked alongside the saints
carrying the sky
and all the stars
between our antlers.

Now Isidorus has put us out to grass
like a herd of old nags.
We cross continents, follow the ancient routes,
shadows of our selves.

Somewhere along the way
like a compelling thought
too often repeated, we've lost
a dimension. The bagpipe-playing boar

has stolen our show.
Flattened between book covers, we are
no more than memories,
pinned down with gold leaf.

Ménage

In my other family
the father's wisdom is never disputed.
He smokes his pipe by the fire,

fishes, tramps over the swamp for diversion.
Mother rocks on her chair,
knitting needles fly like swifts

over black or grey expanses.
She knows how to cast off better than anyone.
In my other family the brothers go out

to hunt deer, sparrow hawk, rabbit,
return laden with booty,
embellish their houses with wives, with trophies:

crows, glass-eyed foxes,
antlers stiffer than branches.
They'll never suffer, my brothers,

the want of red meat.
At night they dream of blue flowers
blue ruin, belladonna, but they remain

steadfast. It's my sisters
in my other family who have been
to the ends of the earth and back,

have seen everything,
give no thought to the past
or the future,

take me at night in silk stockings,
mascara, green stars in my hair,
to the banks of the fast-flowing river,

sing snatches of jazz tunes,
put white bottles on ice for boys
who ride by on motor bikes black as tattoos.

In The Little Building

1

Early in the Boston morning
scores of ballerinas float down
ten heart-breaking storeys
from the Little Building's upper regions,

reach the mezzanine with stop
bells tinkling,
flutter to the nervous light show
of the elevated doors

into the café for pale
wedges of unsweetened grapefruit,
spartan breakfasts,
bitter brew in plastic cups.

Hair pulled tight
in glinting top knots,
blunt-nosed Degas-faces greyer
than the void below the windows,

they breathe monosyllables
into coffees,
toes as bloody
as Cinderella's ugly sisters',

ankles knees in pain from
days of gruelling dancing practice
(oh mummy in Minnesota Dakota
why oh why must I do this?).

Secretly they wrap their feet
in gauze and sticking plaster,
inhale Winston filters in the foyer
with the three Iranian bellhops,

one last taste of pleasure,
then they have to
step again
into their killjoy shoes.

2

After the flicker of lights
and the tinkling bells have subsided
and the ballerinas flown off
to their drill masters

the poets emerge all banter
and chat from their bedrooms,
hirsute as tropical palms and as wrinkled,
in tee-shirts and loose canvas pants,

holding their glistening black cases
tenderly
like newborn infants:
they contain their master pieces,

words and more words
on white pages,
prose or poems in spidery longhand,
funny, airy, tough as nails,

some as roomy as the planet,
some too minute for the naked eye;
but they all are models,
minutely exact replicas

of the great perpetuum mobile
which we usually call the cosmos,
cogs and bolts well-oiled by
midnight draughts of whiskey,

dream machines that rattle until
they produce the one and only
elegant one-liner destined
to wind up the truth once and for all.

And as last resort the poets carry
in a zipped-up secret pocket
the pebbles of silence
tied into an ancient hanky.

LETTER TO SUJATA

*On the occasion of a visit to Paula Modersohn-
Becker's exhibition in Bremen 1996*

Today the sky's like that November day
'96 in Bremen, lowering, grey,
broken by sullen drizzle that soft-pedals
the pavement turning to ice as it falls,
and same as here the sea's just down the road,
unseen but sighing, making its presence felt
like a relation bitter with life in the spare
room. We met near Roland on the square,

neither of us at home in that northern city
of no-nonsense Hanse respectability
whose trademark is not suffering dreamers gladly
or strays like us who hardly
fit in, in uneasy exile, self-chosen but real
nevertheless, both at times painfully made feel
other, outlandish. You, born in India,
graceful poet, who dreamt up in freezing Iowa

tropical gardens for picnics, now live in this
boreal town; (the poet's the one who always
must leave, "saris flapping in the wind", who carries
home "inside her darkness" wherever she goes),
and I, washed-up on this wind-battered island
where the EU and Christ are glove in hand
(where they grudgingly welcome the likes of me,
with my Western-European pedigree

while on more exotic travellers they shut the gate
or respond to their arrival with irrational hate;
they distrust outsiders in both our countries,
pastmasters of log-jam bureaucracies
erecting walls of officialdom marked KEEP OUT
and other such time-honoured pleasantries.
We're better off putting our trust in trees
as you do, Sujata, homesick for bougainvillaeas

the size of elephants, flowering hibiscuses
with their golden-tongued blossoms commonplace
as weeds, for monkey gardens littered by sun,
so when your eyes grow tired of rain
you haunt with your daughter the flower markets
to show her, stunted as bonzais in this climate,
your native plants lined up in plastic pots
specimens from some wintry Lilliput.

We're setting out to see an exhibition
of Paula Becker's, leave the tall patrician
flat-chested houses in their grandeur
close rank on Red-Cross soup tents on the square,
to turn into an unexpected alley
with madcap buildings gone as cracked as Gaudi,
every-which-way the bricks, tiles and glass
stained bluer than the flames of city gas,

fat toads spout water, pixies hold flambeaux,
as daughter Jenny's running rings round us.

And we both feel we, too, have found our feet
at last here in that topsy-turvy street
full of irreverent architectural pranks
in the universal language of high jinks —
imaginary gardens with live toads —
or high art, the real thing not some ersatz.

Inside where the paintings are spread out,
it's like we've walked into a blaze of light
or truth from far benighted places:
no shamming in these bog farmers' faces
or their mothers', who grown gaunt with toil,
we fancy smell of sour milk, damp wool,
little girls in scratchy handspun smocks
holding small children with sullen old looks,

poverty's stamp, thick noses, pale, thin hair,
nothing folksy or mawkish or idealised here,
the big red hands on six-year old kids,
who go out at dawn in their wooden clogs
to milk the cow, the cottager's old wife
in black Sunday silks, and all's alive
with intense colour, rusts, duns and blues,
the young mother, her breasts luminous

in a flame-red bodice as she feeds her baby,
the most sensual Madonna you'll ever see,
"sensual into their very fingertips",
as in 1898 the painter notes.

You say "No one else has brought the light
into their paintings like she did". You're right,
the kitchen-gardens, foxgloves, crockery,
the scotched opaque blues of the sky,

they all are in that natural element
or lit up from within the layered paint,
as though the canvas had been soaked in it.
I think, as Jenny skips from favourite to favourite,
that sometimes in exile it's the deepest wound
to be excluded from the subtext of what's meant,
but here's a language that transcends the otherness,
the painter's true gift is her love, her genius,

how she with courteous and careful eyes
has put her drab and heavy subjects at their ease
and in the centre of their world, that's what
it's all about, speaks to us straight.
We know that poets often make up lies
so they can catch a tail-end of the truth,
but no matter how well and skilfully they do it,
it's as nothing if that ingredient's not in it.

We follow Jenny slowly through the rooms;
the painter gazing out at us from many frames,
her dark brown eyes amused in her young face,
holding her sun-warmed amber necklace,
and dream of monkey gardens, flowering hibiscus trees.

OEDIPUS AND THE SPHINX
(after Acusilaos)

All of us bystanders knew and the great sphinx also knew
that this yellow-eyed club-footed hobbledehoy spelt trouble
hobbling up to the wall where she was enthroned in cruel
                                                              mystery;
he trailed loose dust behind him, his crutch dripped with
                                                                 blood —
of his father it turned out later — and fixed her with a
                                                                  clear
far-away gaze as though taking aim at a boar hunt.

Over a dirty hemp tunic he'd thrown a jerkin of goat's pelt
in the manner of goatherds, two splints on the ankles were
                                                                      tied
blood-stoppingly fast with leather thongs. It was clear to us
and the daughter of Echnida and Ortos that he had nothing
                                                                 to lose.

Raising herself in the light of the setting sun she shook
her rose-tinted top knot and dreadlocks, the oracular bells
                                                                   tinkled,
her great bosom shone like oiled wood, her lion's tail swung
                                                              to and fro.
She'd never seemed more terrifying to us riffraff of Thebes.

When she sang out her riddle he limped closer, groaning as
                                                       though
the pain of knowledge was alone his — he with his crutch —
and answered quietly. She fell sixty feet breaking her skull
on the rocks under her seat where the bones of her victims,
King Kreon's son Haemon among them, lay in grim piles.

We cheered as he went through the gate flanked by two
sphinxes — the Gate of the Blind as it was renamed — went
                                    as heroes will blindly.

On Forgetting

> *Nous ne savons rien de la mémoire, rien, rien.*
> *Sans oubli on n'est que perroquet.* - Paul Valéry
>
> *Jamais n'oublierai cette fumée.* - Elie Wiesel
>
> Forget it. - Colloquial expression

I

It's nothing earthshaking in the beginning,
small lapses, you mislay things, keys, wallets,
forget numbers you ring every day,
increasingly you can't place faces, recall names,
then you begin to take notice:
something is changing, something
is advancing towards you, no bigger yet
than the pin-point of a black star
just over the horizon, still far, still at a safe distance,
hardly making progress but marring the scenery,
the formerly untroubled perspectives.

You ask yourself, is this it, the beginning of the end
approaching almost imperceptibly
like a slight atmospheric disturbance,
the thin edge of the blade? You spot warning signals,
read about memory loss, Korsakov's Syndrome, Alzheimer's,
you discover little that is new and that's mostly
speculation — the journals admit as much —
in your case it's simply a cluster of cells
in your frontal lobe system
slowing down their transmissions, a natural process
at your age. Wear and tear. That's no consolation.

You decide you're going to beat that thing,
not to give in lying down,
set yourself tasks, crosswords, memory drills,
learn historical chess games by heart,
(between Napoleon and one of his generals for instance
checkmated after losing his rook in the 36th move);
you memorise phone numbers, your children's, the doctor's,
but forget your friend's husband's name; addresses,
birthdays you have to look up. Will the day come
when you can't remember the word "apple"? There you are —
past 40, comical, sad, almost tragic, losing your grip on things.

You delve into the past, develop a mania
for keepsakes, memories, like a bloodhound
you track them down — father at the piano,
dead fish floating in dark green water,
GIs smile from the backs of army trucks,
chicken pox, cold wraps, eucalyptus and the scent
of mother's favourite soap —
half-remembered things that you take
by the scruff of the neck and force into the merciless light
of the present. Many things change fast,
you observe politicians and policeman get younger,

increasingly there seems to be less time, fewer emotions,
less love, fun, hope; you're baffled
by the latest technology, you stay in more,
watch chat shows on TV and lie awake at night wondering
what happened and what end your life is rushing towards.

You see your family more often: funerals
are becoming frequent, death strikes closer to you.
You discover how irreplaceable the dead are,
how huge the gaps they leave behind them.
You read books on forgetting. It remains a mystery.

Is the mind simply dumping excess baggage to regain speed
or is it a sort of mental economics,
a jettisoning of odds and ends that weigh it down?
Why then can't it throw off things that once pained it
and are paining still? Why do certain moments
stay fixed in your memory, clear-edged and cutting as ever?
Still drawing blood? You are caught in a dilemma:
unable to forget what you most want to forget,
yet constantly trying to pin down what eludes you.
You feel like a badly tied travel bag
shedding its contents on a bumpy bus ride.

Distraught you take to drinking too much,
desiring what you fear in equal measures,
sometimes you think you've been struggling
up a mountain from which you look down on an ocean
that stretches past the horizon. On the strand
lies the boat you're going to paddle out onto the water.
So after your lifelong battle with keys and phone numbers,
appointments and punchlines,
this is the glistening void you will vanish into.
However, you try to think of that with composure:
sea and boat are familiar metaphysical trappings,

but in one of your nightmares a flame runs along a fuse
through the grass towards you, speeding up
as it comes closer. You wake up sweat-drenched and shaking.
In the dream that follows, two of your dead loves
sit in a garden beside a sunlit river waving to you,
calling in birdlike indistinct voices.
You try to but can't hear what they're saying.
For a while you wonder what it was. Then you forget.
The grand finale is rarely dramatic, rather a little banal: your
hold on things sliding, colours getting dimmer, in the end
only the sound of a fuse crackling in the grass.

II

I, Charles Labussière, nicknamed the Chewer of Paris,
actor and secretarial assistant
to the Committee for Public Safety
during the "terreur",
saved approximately 1500 people from the guillotine
(among them Josephine de Beauharnais,
Napoleon's future wife as well as many actor friends)
by destroying their files.

Afraid of being caught — spies lurked everywhere —
I tore up the documents
printed on the official paper
of the Revolutionary Tribunal and ate them. . .
When my innards rebelled
(pulped rags and wood, gum, animal glue, ink)

*I soaked the pages in a basin of water
kneaded them into papier maché balls
I could carry out in my pockets.
Disguised as an angler fishing for his breakfast
I dumped basketfuls of death sentences
into the Seine at dawn.
After the "terreur" I returned to the stage,
First I was famous, a hero,
"le mâcheur de Paris" people flocked to see,
then I ceased to be news, my career faltered.
An actor friend writes a play about me.
Benefit performances
keep the wolf from the door for a while.
But the play being controversial
is taken off the programmes;
I took to drinking absinthe and vanished
in the bars and flea houses of Montmartre.*

I read this story last April in Vienna,
city of bad memories par excellence
behind its stately façades.
Unseasonal snows fell on Heldenplatz
and a Siberian wind shook the flagpoles.
Below golden domes, stone angels
white as whipped cream flailed their arms
on palace gutters.
We crossed the Danube stopping briefly
to look into the cold stream,
we knew the usual telltale odds and ends
would lie buried in the mud of the river bed:

road signs, party badges, grenade shells
give-away symbols of a sad and ugly past.

We stood for a while thinking we could hear
the river telling her non-stop stories:
that was in the year of the big crash
and later when war came and the embargo started biting
after most of our Jewish neighbours
had vanished — God knows where —
all we ever saw were turnips —
turnip coffee, turnip bread, turnip schnaps;
ah the smell of the bad old days,
typhoid epidemics and a shortage of sulpha drugs
not enough sterile dressings or
painkillers never enough painkillers;
that year mother turned my coat inside out
for the second and last time
the winter was icy
and we couldn't get fuel not one shovel of coal
in the whole of Vienna
remember how that year suicides
were ferried every day across the river
to the Graveyard of the Nameless
in the 11th District. . .

What is this thing — forgetting?
Perhaps you hope that at this moment
someone is tearing up your file,
slowly methodically,
soaking the shreds in a water basin,

carrying them out in his pockets
to dump them into the river,
the magical flood?
Is it asking too much of the executioner
to check through his lists
and not find your name written there,
and, having done his day's work,
to go home to his wife and child?

Last April after I read first about Charles Labussière,
strategist of merciful forgetting
in the city that never forgot
a single one of its victims,
I lay awake and thought of all
the millions who had vanished
thronging the streets
squeezing in past shutters and latches
to make the same urgent request —
to keep their memories alive.

Place, date, name, sentence
the flourish of a signature on pages
torn from files, a verdict
dissolving in water,
slowly drifting downstream.
The angels gesturing to the sky
above dripping gutters
never reach the river.
They're condemned to look on,
petrified by memories of the fall,

while the chewer of Paris,
Charles Labussière in angler's disguise,
an empty basket beside him on the banks of the Seine,
hauls a fish for breakfast from the water.

Some Days

Some days I enter the conference of trees
without knocking.

My worn-out music box
heart needs a new tune:

rustle of rushes
in the ditch with its thin skirt of ice.

Some days the caves sing
of rivers sent out just for me.

But you've made me breathe water,
breathe snow.

I have rolled up my hair
and observed smoke leaping from chimneys.

My heart wants to lie as the rock lies
immovable covered with green

but it splits faster than stone
from the weight of the frail flower hope.

By the old pier I look out for you
when the harbour's aswarm with lights

when boats unload sugars from Barbados
tankers dark liquid from ivory coasts.

At the station with it indecipherable name
and its runaway rail

the stray dogs gather around me
claim me as kin.

I listen for the engine blowing its trumpet
but only cicadas creak their prayer wheels.

Some days I find the right language
for leaf and stone.

Winterland —
where heartland had been.

THE ART JUDGES
(Gabriel Von Max, 1889)

They breeze in from the tops of the trees
headed by a patriarch with sagging belly
and grizzled side-whiskers
and settle on a tea chest marked VORSICHT.

Some pick nits
from each other's pelts,
two regard me with raised eyebrows,
their ancient ironic faces frown,

five have given up on me
and turned towards the gap in the drapes
where the next competitor is unwrapping
a burlesque carving covered in gold leaf.

Two mothers are nursing their babies.
I am waiting for the verdict
while outside the revellers are milling
past the tent in the sunshine.

I know my failings: I let myself be seduced
by words, "blue" for instance or "tree"
instead of making a case,
and there's an overabundance of rivers and seas.

Where are the marital problems,
the primatial condition,
not to mention metaphysics
or the proud origins of the species?

I'll never come up to scratch
in the face of my judges' critical rigour.
At every step they'll stumble
over an owl or a sphinx.

As I sit expecting their pronouncement
any minute now, I hear nothing
except an occasional cough
and the sound of cracking lice.

Angels And Devils

"Spread both your wings, oh Jesus,
embrace your helpless child,
if Satan will devour me
then sing oh angels mild."

Every night my mother used to sing this hymn
by my bedside.

The moment she left he would loom up over me,
his leathery batwings gleamed like radium,
the skin was stretched so hard across the bones
it seemed almost transparent
and I could see ancient cuts and scars
from skirmishes with angels.
Each night the black wings closed around me.
The angels never sang.

On the feast day of St Michael
one of my brothers would take me uptown
to the main square;
in a tense and silent crowd of children,
packed close together as in an underground shelter
when bombs are about to fall,
I stood before the clock tower.
We were there to be taught a lesson:
how to watch a public murder
and that good will triumph over evil.

The moment the small door opened
near the top of the tower
the children began to scream: "Michele, Michele!"
as St Michael and devil lurched out.
Michael, a gust of wind frozen in his golden robe,
held his lance raised and ready.
Beneath his foot the devil squirmed
in a courtier's velvet waistcoat
and puffed short pants,
his tail hung tasselled as a bell rope,
his horns stuck out grotesquely
from his feather cap.
I knew once the killing began
I wouldn't be able to look away.

On each stroke of twelve
Michael stabbed his lance into the devil's belly,
the devil's limbs wriggled,
his jaws opened and shut,
his golden tongue licked the air.
We counted in a crescendo:
"Eins, zwei, drei, vier, fünf, sechs,
sieben, acht, neun, zehn, elf, zwölf!"
Then Michael stiffened
the devil lay dead under his heel,
they turned back
and the door closed behind them for another year.

He came to see me secretly from then on,
I felt his breath on my face in the dark,

he was my bed mate, my confrère, my twin,
he came nightly through the basement door
from which the icy odours of hell were blowing
and every night I'd move aside to give him room.
But gradually we drifted apart,
he faded away among the childhood spectres,
I learned to fear other things.

Then one summer night
he called to me from the garden.
I climbed out the window
and went to where he stood
in a pale green glow between the lilac trees.
I can still feel his ice cold hands on my skin,
his rough hide beneath the gold leaf,
remember his cloven foot
trampling the flower bed,
the feather in his cap shivering
in the night air,
his greedy jaws opening and shutting,
his golden tongue on mine,
our endless fall together.

The Spider

The spider inhabits
the last unlit corners
a few hurried steps from turmoil.

It puts out one foot to test the waters
and you see a shadow glide
over the wall, just there, an inch above the skirting —

like a black vanishing point —
and disappear into the funereal
darkness behind the fridge,

for dark is its element and sinister
its work, its marche funèbre
along the rope drawn

from its own heart
all the way to the abyss.
The spider has been there and back often

waving its eight legs to an inaudible
inner music and in the place of nothing
behold — a dusty grey star

loose ends hooked over the mildewed
branches of a rosebush in October
or straying towards the North

shaky as a compass needle. If
the spider performs feats of hour-long
motionless cliff-hanging or bridging the void

with silk, it's as nothing
compared to its love of geometry. It gives not an inch
on radius even if carried too far

by its hunger for order
which suspends it between two rafters
at the exact ratio of 4/2=10/5.

Having seen enough of the world
it weaves nooses for its prey, lace traps, chiffon
shrouds spread all over the box hedge.

In the end it climbs into its dark nest
folds its symmetrical legs
and dies the lightest death.

The Unicorn

Everywhere the ceremonial brilliance
of summer toned down a shade
or two. The little front gardens
line up in tattered drabs;
hydrangea blooms drooping over the fence
look off-colour and more moth-
eaten than old party hats.

In the MERMAID fishmongers
the kindly blonde assistant
stacks mackerel fillets
with their ink-blue mottles on crushed ice;
her Iranian boss hoses the floor tiles,
blood, entrails, scales
glistening like a thousand
contact lenses flush down the drains
and back out to sea.

The barber shop has been closed for some time.
Behind the shutters the mirror
is filming over with grime,
dust lies everywhere.

Already clippers and scissors
and water basins are tarnished from non-use,
plastic bibs and white coats
dangling from their hooks,
the hairbrushes bristling beside the sinks,

have exchanged their professional briskness
for a limp out-of-service look.

On warm evenings the barber's widow
stands in the door alone
taking in the sun.
She just buried her husband,
aged 81, lollipop man,
card shark, honorary dog warden.
At night a unicorn visits her
in the small hours
when only cats and magpies make
forays to her back garden
and even the revellers on the canal walk
are dead to the world. She states,
he comes to her,
his skin as white and fine as dancing gloves;
he lies down in the weeds
resting his front legs on her lap; he loves it
if she feeds him dandelion heads
or strokes his muzzle
underneath a sycamore.

Early autumn winds sweep the alleys
driving plastic bags and leaves
like ghosts before them.
In her kitchen drawer
the bone-handled knives
lie like soldiers from a past war.

The nights he doesn't come
the dark tongues of the ivy speak to her.

September morning stirs the town
with its iron spoon
and things float to the surface: party men,
schoolgirls, milk trucks on their rounds.
Taxis rush to the suburbs.
The sun arrives with bells and birds,
cleaning machines hoover the curbs;
two JCBs growl past to the swamp.
They circle round and round
on the reclaimed earth
throwing their shovels to heaven as though
they can't believe any of this —
then lower them again to test the ground.

June 18, 1998

High tide and so much water in the heart
of the town; perhaps the sea's wish
to drown the steeples and wash
through attics and treetops has been heard;

see how it surges upstream straining again
to dislodge the boat wreck by the pier,
but it's grown roots into the ground and won't stir,
how it floods inland striving in vain

to reverse the river's course
beyond the third stone bridge, floods uphill
against all reason causing the little spill-
ways and sluice-gates to slosh into canals

and wash over nets and lobster traps,
piled up on the wet mole.
Perhaps someone forgot to turn off taps
and faucets in a distant watery locale,

but that reservoir, too, will run dry,
and eventually, feeling a little blue
and bethinking itself, the tide will withdraw
and carry all the small fry with it out to sea.

No sign of anyone; it's still early,
just seven, although this 18th of June
promises to become "a scorcher of a day"
after weeks and weeks of rain,

the grass on the swamp's just barely
grazed by a maritime breath,
the sun, having mopped up every shred
of cloud and haze on its dawn crusade

makes such a hue and cry above the chimneys,
it alerts the entire world to the joys
of enlightenment, but hoteliers
and undertakers and notaries

in their blind-darkened rooms
squirm away from its dazzling tirade:
one is painting his house blue in a dream,
another's just lost a stack in real estate.

Isn't this morning overdoing it slightly,
so picture-book eager, larger-than-life, freshly
scrubbed and painted, spilling over
with newness and colour like a first primer?

Still no one up yet? Yes, a blue-finned car
noses down Sea Road to the church on the pier,
two young policemen in navy regalia
disembark and march up to the door.

They have left the motor idling over.
Will they confess to some dark felony,
I wonder, or arrest the priest? Their
solemn, expectant air gives nothing away.

Further down river, perfectly drilled
like a battalion of angels at reveille,
eighty, a hundred swans lift their heads
and unruffled and leisurely

glide to the sea wall towards me
in one fluid concerted motion,
eight cygnets in their cinnamon-
mottled plumage among them.

Such a welcome, mute but eloquent;
the birds — not without courtesy — gaze
at me for a heart-stopping second
then veer off slowly on the current.

All salute me today: the million bands
of ripples hardened on the sands,
the clear and saurian-green swell,
sea wrack melting into it like caramel,

benches lined up to face the sea
like dreamy pensioners — WET PAINT signs
on seats bespattered with last night's rains
warning no one in particular — happy but empty,

and the little waves that gurgle and sob
beneath piled-up breakwater rocks,
sing like children scared of the dark
glad to be released into this arch

of light that encircles sea and sky.
And now the world is in full swing.
Three boys crossing the swamp hold a thing
the colour of flame — a kite they're about to fly.

Valse Triste

Vienna leans back
into the last slow curve of the day.
Carriages in the coach yards unhook

and unlace themselves to the evening sun
and in the way of tired refugees
cab horses line up to drink

from a chipped enamel-blue trough.
The day slings its whip over the North Star
shrugs off its green livery

and returns to a secret life
far beyond the outskirts.
In the silence beneath the domed glass

of the imperial hothouse
tropical butterflies flit back and forth.
Like scarves torn loose in a breeze

they flicker over the giant ferns.
What is it that's inscribed on their wings
and keeps them on the move?

In their desire to carry it everywhere
some have ascended to the top panes
spread their wings against the light

and fallen back on ledge and footpath,
brittle and luminous.
"The Jews say they're the souls of the dead",

whispers a young woman.
It's so quiet you can hear water
shimmying over the artificial rocks.

Chrysalises with gargoyle masks
hang in neat rows in the hatchery —
memory knots along strings —

while from the leather flasks of their bodies
spills the crushed Chinese silk of the new
butterfly, millimetre by millimetre.

A dark cloth is shaken out over the squares,
trees in parks and on distant hills open their wings,
trolley cars rise along slopes like flares.

BALLADE
(i.m. of my brother Gerhard)

Ballade, my brother, listen
to only three or four notes more,
clearer than the Indian Ocean
where fish shoals flicker and glow
in the waves for an instant,
flames set alight against darkness,
but darkness is in your ear.

Ballade, my brother,
the rose walls of Ochrid,
city of minarets and spires,
unshuttered themselves to us,
hosted us when the sun went to ground
closing its fiery eye.

Neon signs beckoned to us,
lit up the night
with the outlines of bottles, of starfish.
Ochrid, where pillars grew straight from water
and mosaics were rooted in gold and blue moss.
Boats, winged and black,
swarmed out to the basilica
and, though the lake lay flat as a saucer,
didn't dare cross its treacherous minefields.

Ballade, my brother,
darkness is in your touch,

your fingers can't feel the white and black keys,
the softness of your pillow,
the gentleness of the hand that prepared it.

Never again will we go down stone steps
to the water, cross onto decks
among a summer cargo of travellers,
lean back in deck chairs in diesel fumes,
trust in the rough seafaring turns of phrase
and our arrival together.

We'll never sit at tables in the certainty
the scent of fresh bread spreads
through a kitchen
when the air comes in through windows
like someone breathing soft words,
like promises of love.

Ballade, my brother,
you've left me a music that outlived you
and will outlive my sorrow —
between the pieces an intermezzo
of your calm breathing,
a minute perhaps, no more:
breath you would have such bitter need of now.
Time is measured out
for all of us in such breaths.
I hear and wish I could return it to you,
stop it from stopping.
But your mouth lies among shadows.

Listen to only three or four notes more
of this Ballade, my brother!
All around us darkness
tensed as an ear,
eavesdrops.

Travels With Gandolpho

Do you recall our trip south?
We lay on wooden benches,
ate dried squid from paper bags.
Fields of chillies carpeted the ground
flaming red all the way to the train tracks.
I was aflame, thought of nothing but you.

Time was called — or was it night?
on a dark station platform
below signal posts that someone told us
had been makeshift gallows
they'd hung partisans from during the war.
A kind soul hosed us down,

we drank topaz-coloured wine.
Music came flooding from the wireless,
cantabile, sostenuto.
Handfuls of anise from Nîmes,
light brown mouse droppings.
Can you still see the horses in the arena,

their raised eyebrows and soft eyes,
their curling nostrils?
Would the world be palatable without such airs
and graces?
The prosaic bulls clanked
and jangled inside the stables,

and we drank the bitterest coffee
our worthless money could buy.
The afternoon buzzed with prophetic gadflies.
Grandmother, in the heart of winter,
in her forget-me-not apron,
hesitated between pantry door

and tulip bed. In earthenware jugs
yellow dill feathers bloomed.
She'd almost paid with her life
for the recipe on those long crooked steps
in Odessa. (Years later we tasted the same essence
in a Polish dive east of Notre Dame.)

The hot white liquor with the strange ingredient
made me throw up in the funicular.
You, Gandolpho, held my forehead.
I never loved you as much.
The children below by the river
were jumping in as if it were their future.

Gandolpho's Moods

Gandolpho is two things: never afraid
of life and always in a cello mood;
he climbs on to its rosewood back
and toboggans down the long curving hill of e-flat major.

Sometimes it takes him a day,
half the night, twenty rhapsodies
and every single black and white key
to free all prisoners from the Bastille.

The two French sisters with their lion's heads
polished the same concerto for years
till it shone like brass.
But when they let go
horses stampeded across the Puszta.

Gandolpho tells me: It's hard not to be afraid,
forget those bleak dreams,
meet a friend for the odd truthful chat,
walk on the shaky monkey bridge
of a solo cello suite and cross the void.

Circus

I

In his head he carries a woman
standing at ease with broad hips
and splayed feet. He gives her a yellow apron
and puts small suns all over her scarf.

From inside her belly a child —
or a miniature replica of the woman —
looks out at three blue horses
flying through moon hoops.

A goat lies fast asleep on the roof
while an ostrich plume
is making love to a wreath of smoke
looping around the chimney pot

From the rain barrel
a thousand fallen stars
rise on glass wings.
Where are the horsemen?

II

They bought the biggest egg they could find,
painted the inside with oxblood
and threw a few sparkles
against the walls.

Then they took a long hair
tied a golden woman to it
and suspended her
from the top.

They tilted its axis
and set it spinning.
Finally they called in the clowns
the sawdust, the violins, the crowds.

It'll take her a lifetime
to find her feet.

III

On entering the tent
you must leave your heart and face
behind in the cloakroom.

IV

The shooting star gallery has been set up.
Clowns in drab fatigues
nail bits of luminous skin
to the tent walls.

All the stars going round
will be shot down one by one.

You are guaranteed to get your turn.

In the end the skin
will be delicately monogrammed
with your name.
The bards will be working the rifles.

V

The frog prince was kissed
by the Lippizaner horse
and turned into a cephalopod.
It took no one by surprise.

VI

The physician of transformations
has been called
to the poets' caravan:
one of them has changed himself
into an imaginary number.
But the physician can do less than nothing
about it.

VII

The spider flies from joist to joist
just below the tent roof,

deftly ties up her safety net
to ensure the audience
won't break their skulls
when they fall out of their seats.

VIII

The director has absconded.
His chair has been empty
for as long as the debate
on his absence has been going on.

Every other year
some one claims it with fire and drums,
divides lion tamers, hunger artists,
stable boys, frog princes, clowns etc.
into enemy camps.

Pro-factions try to wipe out
the contra-faction and vice versa.

Sooner or later they're all
brushed out and dumped
while blood trickles
from the trumpets
into the dust of the arena.

IX

The fat lady and the strong man
are getting married.
Turtle doves fly from the guests' sleeves
and fan out to form
a fluttering white baldachin
over their heads.
The violins chirp melodies full of pink bubbles,
the double bass weeps the blues.

In Duiche Iar

The fields were no larger than the green envelopes
our dead-and-gone Greek teachers used
to post obloquies to our parents.

We climbed stone walls, got lost in a maze.
Round every corner we feared the minotaur
might come crashing through brambles

but, as luck would have it, we met face to face
only the serene local bull,
a youngster with six female dependants.

In Duiche Iar light dripped, rocks and tarmac
glittered from thousands of punctures,
the mountains were studded with pin points of silver.

Thigh-deep in marsh reeds we watched the Atlantic
turn over once more on its back.
I don't know why the crows reminded me of seminarians,

maybe because they were huddled together,
celibate and black, in the one tree
not blown back to front by the storm

which crashed raging against a bolted gate
somewhere beyond the hills,
bundled us through the graveyard

where the dead in their coffin ships
were slowly sinking towards bedrock.
We were amazed at an old sand stealer

who with his donkey was busy rearranging the planet,
a job more futile, we thought,
than that of King Sisyphus.

On Duiche Iar strand the sea rolled up
the scroll with its signature in fresh blue ink,
left urchins shells dotting the shore

white as fairy skulls and as bald,
we could see the stitch holes of elfin embroidery
where their needlework was unpicked.

In Duiche Iar we discovered dogs own six senses or more
and all the boreens. One appeared to us
out of thin air, tailed us wherever we went

to shield us from harm, barked at anything
that moved, our shadows, the neighbour's labrador,
a tractor rattling past. We knew well

we couldn't take a step without her
and submitted, counting our blessings,
this windfall of kindness on such rocky ground.

Let our companions on our travels always
be like her with her wind-blown coat
in true local colour, black and white,

her tilted left ear and her dissimilar eyes,
one a deep liquid brown,
the other blue and changeable as her native sea.

Her dark eye saw a future fraught with danger,
her blue eye looked into a world
where metamorphoses were commonplace as rocks,

gods walked on hindlegs, stars fell into tin pails
and the ends of the earth
rested on the shoulders of mongrels.

Berlin Notebook

> *There is no escape from yesterday because yesterday has deformed us or been deformed by us.* — Samuel Beckett

> *History is like a text on which the past has stored images as on a light-sensitive plate. Only the future possesses the chemicals necessary to develop the image in all its clarity.* — Walter Benjamin

I

Fatherland

Drawing board avenues in straight
double rows line up for the victory parade.
On his golden horse the general rides in,
his head filled with war. It is 1914.

Hussars from the barracks clack down the streets
in twos and twos, strait-laced as rhyming couplets,
wave follows plumed wave, such young blood
trying to steal a march on death.

Flights of steps lead underground
guarded by mendicant rainbow girls
cowering beside their Cerberus hound.

MORGENPOST pages tumble past in whirls,
the sky is closed as the grave. Skirls
of hot air rise from a subway vent.

II

Graves

The graveyard wall near Mehringdamm,
grapeshot pocked from street battles in '45
is gaudy with graffiti: WAR TO WAR
9th OF NOVEMBER NEVER FORGET
NAZIS OUT
WE LOVE GORBI
the work of the Kreuzberg historiographers.

E.T.A. Hoffmann lies here;
under a pall of dusty ivy
he sails the underground seas
with a supply of dream elixirs and automatons.

The earth is riddled with rabbit warrens
crossing the tracks of the dead.
One rabbit flung on the footpath
limp as an inside-out fur glove.
Black flies have settled on it
with perfect esprit-de-corps.
I'll always remember how its eyes
stared me out.

III

Nightingale

It's the beginning of May in Potsdam beside Berlin, midnight
after a mild day. The golden palaces stretch their limbs in a

wide green park. The moon rocks in its blue cradle and all the marble nymphs abandon their plinths to dip a toe in the scrolled basin of the fountains. The kings are long dead and buried below laurel scents, and so are their legendary army of giants.
I wander through the prim and Prussian little streets, along tree-lined avenues and onto the railway bridge. A lonely nightingale starts to sing, the first I have ever heard. The old music box city throws open its stained glass doors on the tinkle and chime of bells and gongs. Someone steps up to me with a white light and demands to see my credentials. Below me in the tangle and order of tracks a goods train is right on course, engines move to and fro. Down there my old life continues while here on the bridge I have started something new. The nightingale doesn't hold back, it goes straight for the heart. It lifts its voice like a hammer and drives home nail after ringing nail.

IV

Bunkers

No other place seems so versed in death and water —
so many graveyards, so many rivers, canals, watertowers
and the soil light to the spade, liquid almost.
A special gate in every street for refugees, asylum seekers,
another admits winter only sailing down from Siberia on its
                                                      ice plough.

Moses ben Mendel arrived here and paid his toll
before he could enter the city to write
on the immortality of the soul and the existence of God.
"Today two goats plus one Jew from the East
whom I renamed Mendelssohn", notes the gate keeper.

The city's been given a brave new heart
of glass, marble and steel.
Everywhere there are skyscrapers
like polished crystals dropped from the air.

Only a few steps below the surface, below the old centre,
there are the places of death, the bunkers
and bloodied cellars with their despairing graffiti
and the catacombs of murder running with tears.
And in me, too, as I stroll through the glittering streets
one dark cavern opens into another and another.

V

Roland's Song

Our young neighbour Lily
crouches on the landing outside her door,
four flights high at minus 10°
smoking in twilight,

lovely in black-out fabrics
with her bomb-shelter hair
on end and jay-blue,
eyes deep in kohl,

from her fingertips fall embers
into the ash pail, rises smoke.
Icy December draughts rise
from the coal cellars,

yards flow into yards
spilling over with gloom
through frosted glass fan lights.
Everywhere on the yard walls:

WE LOVE YOU LILY!
"Mene tekel" says Lily and inhales deeply,
then: "It's criminal
what we have done to death".

Sam from Harlem in the last
but one tenement blows golden
streamers across to her on his saxophone,
sends his heartbeat after them.

Often shadowy boys shouldering trouble
black dogs at heel, climb the stairs
call for Lily, their ghost train eyes
bitter with longing.

Cool on her landing
they'll love her
drink stuff of high voltage, smoke
the forbidden leaf,

She's a student of death;
she'll tell them how Roland took leave
of his loyal companions
folded his hands on his breast and died calmly,

how coffins used to be stored in trees,
market was held in the graveyards,
and the time will come
when all we will have to lose is the world.

VI

Kreuzberg Nuptials

I look down six stories into the dark
shaft where bins and bikes are tethered
and a blue tricycle lies on its side.
The lunette in the disused backyard factory
shimmers with a dirty white light.
I can almost read the pre-war
lettering above the door:
MEYER maybe, or MEYERBEER.

I look up past twenty five smoke stacks
and seven long roof tops, occupied by pigeons
standing in crooked lines
with their backs
to the green neon cross
of the Christian Hospice

that hangs above us all. On the opposite
side the crescent of a day moon
is wedged between two chimney pots
and a star above it, a glittering stud
in the grey Berlin sky. The red
warning lights are going on and off
around the red brick neck
of the church across the Landwehr Kanal,
and nothing has prepared me
for this outburst of cymbals,
these clashing bells and gongs
and the drawn-out tones
of eastern clarinets.

All the music in the world
seems to have gathered down there,
a crowd has appeared from nowhere,
little girls in gold and garnets,
mothers weighty in silks,
old men with embroidered caps
and a group of Armani-suited young sharps
who clap their hands and chant
as the bride is carried
through the courtyard,
out through the door whose
wings are spread wide,
out to the flashing limousines.

In the sudden silence below
confetti swirls round and settles
like colourful sediment.

The peak of Mount Ararat hovers
above the city and the shore
of the Marmara Sea has come
a few blue leagues nearer.

VII

The Nightsinger

When the insomniac next door finally stops pacing,
the last cars slip into anchorage,
the last windows erase themselves
from the *Gründerzeit* façades opposite,

when night rains fall from the top tiers
of the summer theatre above Berlin,
and each street lamp swims
in a wavery orange nimbus,

when all alarms are silenced,
the night is a great ear
pressed close to the heart of the city,
and we sleep high up under a pre-war roof,

with nothing between us
and the vast outdoor auditorium,
its aisles and mute orchestra pit,
but a few bricks, planks and tiles,

we often wake after he's already gone past
a block or two, his voice still in our dreams:
a full bass or baritone, the right touch
of vibrato, operatic but not excessively so,

light in the high notes: *Tosca,*
Il Trovatore, The Magic Flute,
a solo melody that rises and descends
past fire walls, chimneys and gutters,

past the assembled polished utensils of the night.
We listen, the houses bend and listen
to this song coming from beyond parks
and bunkers, concert halls,

apartment blocks, graveyards,
weaving in and out of the night sounds
high above the old divisions, losses, hopes and the new.
In the gods we think of him testing the freedom of the city

with each breath, each crescendo, think of blue
water rising to our attic and sweeping us
all the way to Brazil. We've heard him before,
here and there, turning up at exactly the hour

when ears are most receptive; you recall
Baptist hymns trailing round Boston Common at 3 a.m.,
barely audible above the ocean howl
of traffic, unquelled by police sirens;

once at Ostkreuz, Tristan on a bench between tracks
going all the way to middle B
beside himself with potion and desire,
and not long ago by the Eglinton canal, you swear,

you overheard him sing the Mikado in a scruffy overcoat
to an audience of waterfowl.
Call him a lunatic, you say,
but unless you know

he still wanders the city to his own song till daybreak
you can't feel right in a place.
Unless you know that he still has the freedom
to sing as pleases him, we to listen.

VIII

Amber

The train rushes along below the water table.
We sit stiffer than puppets
submerged in darkness behind saffron windows
with our papers and briefcases.

A woman fingers a pendant — amber
enclosing petals, tiny insects.
(Sunday silks, the perfumes
of resin and lavender,
mother's necklace from holidays
at Travemünde).

At Unter den Linden we climb out of the earth
into the blonde October light.

In the flea markets Polish women sell amber,
strings of beads polished
to the colour of light honey
or opaque and reddish as pollen,

some hawk amber eggs
the size of hand grenades.
They hold them in their palms tenderly
as if they could blow up a storm,
as if the sea could come to reclaim them.

Notes:

Letter to Sujata:
Paula Modersohn-Becker, 1876-1907, painter and member of the Worpswede artists' colony near Bremen.

Rhinoceros:
This poem was kicked off by Brian Bourke's series of rhinoceros paintings based on Pietro Longhi, the Oxford Bestiarium, José Louis Borges, Hildegard von Bingen, Isidore of Seville and Shakespeare. Section VI refers to Albrecht Dürer's 1515 woodcut of a rhinoceros according to a Dutch sailor's description.

On Forgetting:
I am indebted to Harald Weinrich's *Lethe, Kunst und Kritik des Vergessens* for the story of Charles Labussière.

Circus:
This is loosely based on Jay Murphy's paintings and drawings of the Florilegio Circus.

Berlin Notebook:
II: 9th November; both the date of Kristallnacht (the Night of Broken Glass) 1938, and German unification in 1990.
E.T.A. Hoffmann, 1776-1822, German romantic poet.
IV: Moses Mendelssohn, 1729-1786, philosopher of the enlightenment and grandfather of Felix Mendelssohn-Bartoldy.
V: The poem refers to *L'homme devant la mort* by Philippe Ariès.